1970305

C000145285

Through the Eyes of a **Dolph**

Through the Eyes of a Dolphin

Copyright © 1996 by Liliana Saca. All rights reserved.

ISBN 0-9650530-8-3

Printed in the USA on recycled paper.
No part of this publication, with the exception of brief quotations, may be reproduced in any form without written permission.

FIRST EDITION
Published by
Spaceframe Press
Box 2, 187 Bahia Circle
San Rafael, California 94901

Book Design & Copy Editing: Sharon Skolnick
Cover: VISIGRAF/Visionary Graphics
Author's Photo: DINO, San Francisco, CA
Dolphin Photos: Liliana Saca
Cover/Back Photos of Author and Friend: Leticia Padilla
Author's Logo Design: Cathrine Miloslavich

Through the Eyes of a Dolphin

An Inner Journey
Which Can Only
be Approached
in the
Imagination ...
Beyond the
Mind,
Experienced in
the Heart and
Recognized by
the Soul

Liliana Saca, M.A.

SPACE FRAME PRESS
SAN RAFAEL, CALIFORNIA

Through the Eyes of a Dolphin

I *dedicate this book*
with all my heart to my family.
For all the love, support & sacrifices ...

Mom and Dad,
I *am proud to be your daughter!*

Jona, *my angelic sister,*
thank you for always being there for me!

I *also dedicate this book*
to my **Spirit Guides,**
for their constant guidance and wisdom,
thanks for never giving up on me.

... and of course to the **Dolphins,**
thanks for sharing your messages!

Through the Eyes of a **Dolphin**

Acknowledgments

Special thanks to:

Tish, my best friend,
thank you for your love, support and believing in me!
I will always treasure our friendship forever.

John, you will always be a special part of my life,
thank you for helping me find my strength.

Esencia, you opened my eyes
to a new reality and for that I will
be forever grateful.

Lita, my soul sister,
thank you for being my conscience.

Doña Josefa, my beautiful grandmother,
thank you for your sincere love.

To my grandfathers, Thomas and Emeterio,
and to my Grandmother, Carlota,
your spirits will always be inside me.

Peter, for inspiring me with your
respectable life accomplishments,
thank you for reminding me that I, too,
can accomplish what my heart desires.

Sharon, thank you for
taking on this project and
helping me bring one of my dreams
into reality.

A Note:

There are numerous books written about dolphins; informative myths and stories about dolphins, research and scientific books about dolphins, dolphin channeled books, and even books on future inter-species communication with dolphins.

We have no understanding of living in their world as much as they have an understanding of ours. Until we can discover a way to communicate with these magnificent beings, we might as well simply under-stand and reflect on the dolphins just as they are: not in a scientific way, but as beings sharing the universe with us.

Through the author's thorough design, this book is projected in a different light. *Through the Eyes of a Dolphin* shares the author's personal reflections on these exotic beings and supports these insights with research and credible documented studies.

TABLE OF CONTENTS

ix

Foreword

by Ashleea Nielsen
(Author, *Dolphin Tribe: Remembering the Human - Dolphin Connection*, Dancing Dolphin Press, 1994)

It is very clear to me ... consciousness is attempting to communicate with us at this period in history. Consciousness is not using our rules, our languages. Its attempts are through other means, such as crop circles, dreams and telepathic messages from dolphins and whales. As we learn to communicate with this consciousness, our perception of reality is shifting. Ultimately our reality itself will change.

We so-called Earth Humans who operate in the beta-mode for the most part don't get it that blasting radio waves into space or putting sound frequencies in the water via boom - boxes or teaching a dolphin sign language isn't working. Our lesson right now is to establish a language of the common ground. This is of paramount importance.

Through the Eyes of a Dolphin takes you into Liliana's common ground, her personal myth. She has opened up to the vaster consciousness and valiantly dived in to explore the world of synchronicities, symbols and metaphors. She has made the connections that are necessary to assist in the creation of unity consciousness. As she states, "Perhaps our communal consciousness can also enable us to communicate everything 'all at once,' creating a group mind in constant harmonious contact with all." Liliana and I share the same dream. We are pod-ners, to be sure!

Unity consciousness has been initiated on Earth. The unity consciousness grid is now in place, and once our consciousness reaches a certain level, all our problems will be solved, and healing will occur. This new consciousness is here, without a doubt!! Liliana's book is a valuable contribution to humankind's wake-up call! As you swim through the pages of this book, realize that Liliana's journey is not unlike your own. We are all going home ... and together!

— Ashleea Nielsen
Maui, Hawaii
November 27, 1995

Through the Eyes of a Dolphin

Introduction

In the past several years I have in a sense led two lives: a public life building a career as a professional executive, and a private life in which I embarked upon my own metaphysical self study program. My primary focus for the past fifteen years has been my quest for metaphysical knowledge. My journey for personal, spiritual growth encompassed numerous books and articles, various seminars, many workshops and culminated in a Master's Degree. The search for myself and the years of theoretical research are now the foundation of my book.

Ideas about myself, others and what is going on around me constantly run through my mind. This is how I shape my life — my expectations. Everything around me — television, radio, newspapers, magazines, advertisements, books, etc. — affects me. The symbols and metaphors are well-hidden, yet play an important role in the process of my consciousness.

Symbolism creates a new line of force in my psyche and can change my inner attitude and outer behavior. Symbols link together one state of my consciousness with another, bringing clarity in some way and heightening my reality. The dolphins are my personal living symbol. For me they denote reverence, awe and mystery. The dolphins' mystique moves me into some kind of direction — moving me to action and pointing me into the "new," the unknown.

Metaphors are especially powerful stories. When I use metaphors — saying that one thing is something else — what I am saying is *literally* untrue, but it tells me something very true. It shows a truth of my world. Myths and metaphors are great liberators of the soul which connect us with the invisible flow of life.

Joseph Campbell, the great mythologist, stated that fairytales were expressive of consciousness, and that original religious stories and myths, which were "truth," brought us to higher consciousness. "The mythogenic zone today is the individual in contact with his own interior life, communicating through his art with those 'out there.'"[1]

In writing *Through the Eyes of a Dolphin*, I had
to discover the internal sources of my own story.
I had to ask questions about what actually is the
story of my life — not just what happened to me
but what kind of character I was within this
myth. Through visualization and the power of
metaphor, I discovered additional insights within
me. My credential for speaking about dolphins is
simply my passion, connection and unconditional
love for them. The Dolphin Consciousness has
always intrigued me since I was a child.
Throughout my life I have been fortunate to have
encountered these exotic beings. I could be on a
cruise ship, sailboat, rubber raft or on the beach,
when they have unexpectedly appeared. Now
they even appear in my dreams. There is a mysterious connection that even I myself cannot
explain.

   Through the Eyes of a Dolphin will take you into
my personal myth, my magical dream journey.
I believe that there are other dimensions beyond
the three-dimensional world model. I can tap
into another dimension in my dream state, and
this is where I interact with the Dolphin
Consciousness. *Through the Eyes of a Dolphin*
is literally alive with signs, symbols and

metaphors. Approach my inner journey with an open mind, use no judgment, and just allow the symbols and metaphors to speak for themselves. Reflect on my interpretation of the spirit of the dolphins subtle messages, and simply absorb the information that is beneficial to you.

My intent is to share my personal truths. You will come to understand why I have such an intense love, awe and sense of wonder for these exotic beings. The nature of their presence, etheric and physical, deeply touches my heart, for they express a simple but true message of cooperation and intunement with life.

chapter one

DREAM

WAKE-UP CALL

One weekday morning I jumped out of bed to find the words reverberating over and over in my head, "Wake-up, lighten up, be freer, play more, life is too short!" What an unusual dream ... what was it all about? I know it must have been a very intense dream, for my heart was racing and every cell in my body was pulsating. I sat back down on my bed to try to recapture my dream, but it was too late. All I remembered was repeating the words, "Wake-up, lighten up, be freer, play more, life is too short!"

I turned to my nightstand to look at my alarm clock. How unusual, I thought, I awoke one minute before my alarm was set to go off at 7:00A.M.. Ordinarily I slap the snooze button two or three times before rolling out of bed to start my day. Although I started my

1

morning a half an hour early that day, I still followed the usual routine.

My automatic coffee maker had already brewed my coffee. I poured myself a cup, took a shower and got ready for work. I walked to my rented garage space a block away. I then drove to my office and its parking garage. As I walked from the garage to my office building, a strange feeling made me suspect that this day was going to be different. The trees around me seemed to droop and the energy around me felt somewhat low. Fleetingly I recalled that the last time I'd had a similar feeling was the morning before the big earthquake hit San Francisco in October of 1989. As quickly as these thoughts entered my mind, however, they soon dissipated as I approached the entrance to my office build-ing. Back in my regular routine, I greeted the receptionist "Good morning," opened my office door, threw my bag on the chair and headed straight to the coffee room.

John, one of my business partners, was in the coffee room. We greeted each other and began a business discussion. In the midst of

2

our conversation, we heard a faint scream from Christy, our office manager, "Get out of the building ... NOW!" I heard her screaming these words over and over as they rang louder and louder in my ears. John and I looked at one another and knew instantly that a bomb had been found in our building. Unfortunately, our offices are directly below the federal building. Although there have been several false bomb evacuations in our building, somehow I knew this one was real. As John and I ran towards the emergency exit, I suddenly remembered my purse: Everything important to me was in my purse and it was still in my office. I stopped dead in my tracks and headed back to the office; I grabbed my purse and immediately ran back towards the emergency exit. As I headed across the street to get as far as I could from the building, I heard an explosion. Amidst the crowd of people frantically exiting the building, I somehow managed to meet up with John again. Relieved but bewildered by my delayed arrival, John questioned my sudden disappearance. I lowered my eyes and had no reply. I was embarrassed to tell him the truth. He then noticed I was clutching my purse tightly. With a look of disbelief, he shook his head and said no more.

John and I just stood there, dazed and confused about what had just happened. I felt immersed in a thick cloud where everything moved in slow motion. Though I was surrounded by chaos, I remained still. Suddenly fire trucks, police cars and ambulances were swarming around us. A flood of sirens and lights filled the air. The deafening sounds were inaudible to me. The flashing lights were invisible to me. I was numb and felt no emotion. Could this be a sign from the universe telling me to stop and take inventory of my life?

After what seemed like hours after the incident, John tapped me on the shoulder and pointed in the direction of the garage. We walked to the garage in complete silence. As we passed a nearby office building, a group of "business suit and power-tie" executive types emerged from

4

a power meeting and walked by. One of them commented that we looked as if we had just lost a war. Shocked by his "unawareness" of what had just occurred around the corner, John and I both looked at him with blank expressions and did not even respond to his remark. He then gave us a strange look, shrugged his shoulders and hurried back to his group.

Once again, John and I continued on our regular route toward the parking garage. As we neared the entrance, a white van approached. I moved out of the way to let the vehicle pass, causing John and I to separate. However, instead of turning right towards the entrance, I continued straight. I heard John's voice directing me back to the garage, so I turned back to head in the right direction. I thought to myself, "How strange it was for me to go the wrong way — after all, I have walked this path a million times." As I passed the white van, I noticed that the windows were open and a purse was lying on the passenger seat. Should I run after the woman who parked the van and tell her that she had left her purse unattended? "What if somebody takes it? I guess that's her problem, not mine," I thought. As I caught up with John, I clutched my purse tightly, happy to have it.

As we approached our cars, John and I exchanged our usual good-byes as if nothing extraordinary had happened that day. Back on auto-pilot, I got into my car, started the ignition and headed towards my other parking garage a block from home. As I walked the usual path to my door, I noticed a huge crowd at the marina park. I knew from the presence of numerous television vans, posters and media personalities that a big event was taking place. The event was a promotional party for the television show "Bay Watch." It occurred to me that it just did not seem right to have all this extensive media coverage over such a superficial event, while not one single media crew was evident after the tragic bomb explosion.

Totally preoccupied by my thoughts, I realized I had walked past my home. Correcting my oversight, I headed in the right direction. Once again as I went, I unconsciously managed to pass my house again. I have walked this same path a million times. I really must be losing it. I passed it up again and again ... for the life of me I could not find my way home. I knew for certain I was on the right street; then I realized I could not recall my address. Frustrated and confused, I opened my purse and reached for my wallet. How bizarre — I had to pull out my driver's license to look up my address. I looked at the address on my driver's license and noted the number of the house in front of me. I was only a few houses away. Finally I reached the front of my home. I noticed there was a bookstore on the corner. Strange, I never realized that store ever existed. Had it always been there?

I pulled out my keys to open my door and found it would not open. I stepped back to look at the address and confirmed I was definitely at the right place. I tried the key again but still it did not open the door. Confused, I looked around. How strange, I never noticed that all the homes looked alike. Trying to find logic in another bizarre situation that day, I concluded that I must be at the wrong house. My house key must open one of the other doors. All I needed to do was to try my house key on each of the doors on my block. Suddenly all the keys fell off my key chain. I scrambled to pick them up. I picked up all of the keys that had fallen except for my house key. I searched everywhere retracing my steps, but I could not find my house key.

I could not take it anymore. I was on the verge of tears. I was frustrated and confused from the pattern of bizarre events that had befallen me that day. For the first time, I lost it and broke down. I finally allowed myself to release all the emotions that had built up inside me that day, and probably many others.

Was I dreaming? Was this really happening to me? I walked this path a million times. Was I really lost? How could I be lost? I could not find my way. I could not find my home. I could not find my key. Yet all I cared about was my meaningless purse!

chapter two—

IN
SEARCH
OF
PASSION

Abruptly I jumped out of bed, repeating the words, *"Wake-up, lighten up, be freer, play more, life is too short!"*

That dream contained so many symbols and metaphors for me with such intensity that my life from that day forward was never the same. I have all the components of what others would view as a so-called "normal" life. I live comfortably, have a respectable professional career, a loving family and caring friends. I walked around masquerading as content beneath the mask. I knew something was missing and felt empty inside. My passion for life was dead. That dream was a wake-up call for me to rediscover my passion.

Unfortunately, I had a major dilemma which prevented me from finding this passion. Doubt, that was my dilemma — that nagging doubt in my mind. How could I leave a secure and comfortable life to find this passion? What would happen to me if I leave all this? What if I cannot find this passion? Was this dream giving me permission to release my doubt and free myself from my so called "normal" life? After all, I did feel empty inside. I was slowly dying inside. What did I have to lose? There must be a better way of living my life, to live my life in its best meaning, not to live my life in its ultimate end. As hard as it was to persuade my logical mind to let go and leave my comfort zone, I made my decision. I gave myself permission to find my passion. Giving myself permission, I suddenly felt a gigantic burden lifting from my heart.

Truly, my favorite pastime is being by the ocean. For me, the ocean is a secret, beautiful and peaceful place. The ocean draws me in times of loneliness and in times just "to be." The musical sounds of the waves, the smell of the salt air, the grains of sand massaging my feet and the soothing calmness of the space help me find my inner peace. When I am near the ocean I can forget the world around me. It is where for a few hours I can feel as if I were alone at the beginning of time. The ocean is my special place, where I can communicate with that living spirit within me.

So, here I am on Kauai, the "Garden Island," a magical island that I seem to have an unexplainable connection with subconsciously. Kauai might be a perfect place for me to find my passion. I am now driving towards my favorite beach, following the road until it ends on the west side of the island. Finally no more paved roads, I am leaving the material world behind, driving through a maze of sugarcane fields. Peeking through the tall sugar cane, I can see the dark jagged peaks appear to my right. This area is still as I remember it to be — so exhilarating and so colorful. Different shades of green of the trees and bushes and the black rocks mixed with deep red from the volcanic soil. As I reach the end of the road and emerge from the base of the cliffs, I can finally see my special place, the beach of "Polihale."

What a spectacular view! Imagine a tri-colored ocean as the backdrop connecting with the never-ending blue sky and the golden sand stretching out to eternity. The cliffs look like exotic towers; I wonder if some lost civilization ever lived here? With my picnic lunch, beach mat and sun tan oil, I am off to find my passion.

* * * *

I sat quietly looking out into the ocean. I decided to view myself in a different way. I wanted to see myself from an outside perspective, to see myself as another being.

I watched myself going through my everyday walk of life with detachment. It was quite amusing to discover that I have been wandering around aimlessly to who-knows-where. As an observer, I realized that I really never knew who I was. The person I viewed was living childishly, the "way of illusion." She did not realize what she was doing. She lived a life of "practicality" and "complexity." She was obviously obsessed with power, progress, time and egotism.

She lived in a progressive culture, a futuristic world created by high technology. Her culture built impressive modern highrise buildings and created spectacular skylines, panoramic bridges and grand, expansive highways. It even created man-made imitations of nature to beautify its land. Its technology was quickly advancing to make way for the computerized information highway era.

Viewed from afar, this world was truly impressive. However, deep inside I knew

that this backdrop was a beautiful mask to hide the power and desire to control everything. I knew that if I looked behind the mask, this so-called magnificent world which her culture created was slowly deteriorating its land, poisoning its oceans and ultimately diminishing its spirits.

My thoughts were suddenly interrupted by a strange sound. As I sat on the beach contemplating these deep thoughts, I heard a strange yet familiar sound. I could see from my vantagepoint behind the rocks and above the sand a lively group of dolphins heading toward the beach in my direction. I sat on the beach for what seemed like hours, enjoying this spectacular performance. All my problems and worries disappeared as I watched the dolphins playfully frolicking in the ocean.

One dolphin in particular caught my attention. This dolphin had very deep, passionate and intense eyes. I named the dolphin Namaka (NAH-MAH-kuh), the Hawaiian word for "the eyes." How gracefully, playfully and truly childlike Namaka moved. Once again our eyes met, and I felt a strong electrical, magnetic connection with this exotic being. As if our minds connected, Namaka broke away from the pod and headed closer to shore in my direction. Namaka looked directly into my eyes, and I could tell he was trying to communicate with me. I heard a faint voice, but it was coming from within my mind.

"That's it, I am really going crazy," I thought. "This does not appear to be logical." I recognized the voice to be that of Namaka, yet I never heard him speak. How could this be possible? Over and over in my mind I heard the phrase, "Open your heart and leave your logical mind behind." Again our eyes connected, and I felt instant peace and trust. Namaka's voice in my mind told me it was time for me to play and be free. Namaka invited me to join him on

an inner journey to see the world through his eyes. The playful spirit in me wanted to see the world through his eyes, but my pragmatic side reminded me that it was impossible. First of all, I cannot stay out in the ocean for too long because my home is on the land. Secondly, I need to breathe air.

Aware of my thoughts, Namaka advised me to "Wake up, lighten up, be freer, play more, life is too short! As you opened your heart to me, leave behind your logical mind, and trust. Release all your emotional and mental clutter that is surrounding you. Hold on to my dorsal fin and take a deep breath."

Looking into Namaka's eyes, feeling pure peace and trust, I accepted the invitation. I took hold of Namaka's dorsal fin and took a deep breath. As I released my breath all my mental and emotional clutter was released from my body. I felt so much lighter. I was ready to descend to the deeper waters, unafraid, breathing comfortably and anticipating an enjoyable adventure to the unknown with my new-found friend.

17

chapter three—

DOLPHIN INNER MIND JOURNEY

My journey begins ...

****

*I am swimming through the
Ocean Consciousness with
Namaka,
conscious of each breath.
Surrounded by the beautiful, tri-colored ocean.
Caressed by the water as I soak in the magnificence,
I lift my face to take in the heavenly blue sky above,
as the sunrays softly warm my face.
I feel so ALIVE!*

****

*The ocean was much more than I imagined —
a living reality, supporting and loving.
I made a conscious choice to play in it,
enjoying it to the fullest,
and loving it as I had felt its
love for me.*

18

Suddenly, spirited shadows draw quickly our way,
It's a pod of dolphins, Namaka's friends,
coming to join us on our journey.
They spring out into the mystical air of sunshine,
bringing joy and laughter to the realm,
descending back into the ocean,
into the never-ending, flowing embrace of the ocean.

Playing and laughing with my new-found friends,
content to be where I was,
self doubt and guilt had gone,
I knew I had no limits.
What a difference ... personal freedom.
I feel so FREE!

****

Namaka and his friends are taking
me on an inner journey,
a journey deep into the Ocean's Consciousness,
to learn more about the world through their eyes.

We descend to the deeper layers of the ocean,
breathing comfortably, feeling unafraid,
causing my consciousness to ascend
to a more clear awakened state.
As we sink methodically into the ocean,
I become conscious of the energy and power
available to me.

****

We dove deeper through the greater
layers of the ocean,
experiencing harmonic colors
and kaleidoscopic sounds,
the intense energy of the vibrations
penetrating my awareness,
energies that were more felt than seen.

We began to spiral down,
deeper into the center of the ocean,
entering an entirely different world,
traveling through an energy vortex,
whirlpool waves of consciousness
created by the dolphins,
rejuvenated by the magnetic and
electrical energies all around,
crossing the passageway where time stands still.

A dimension of time —
a reality of time not linear.
We were entering another
dimension of consciousness
where past, present and future are one,
a world where land and sea have no partition,
a world no longer a place of black or white,
but a place of black that is white.
A world no longer representative
of male or female,
but combining the two into a mysterious whole.
A world where Body, Mind and Spirit
form an eternal now.

I began experiencing being a part of everything,
sensing the oneness of the universe.

We dove to even greater depths,
deeper into the center of the Ocean's Consciousness.
We reach the bottom of the ocean.
Illuminating auric glows of purple and
green hues embrace the realm,
providing me with warmth and energy,
filling me with an over abundance of peace.

****

Namaka connects with my thought waves:
"The Dolphins' Consciousness is not something
that is rational,
it is not something that can be
analyzed and solved.
The Dolphins' Consciousness is something
that can only be approached in your imagination,
beyond your mind,
experienced in your heart,
and recognized by your soul.
Listen, not with your ordinary ears,
but with the ears of your spirit.
Listen, find that peaceful stillness
that is deep inside you,
the magic of life within you,
the grace of life itself."

(Namaka picks up a crystal and
places it in my hand)

"This crystal is a gift to you from the ocean.
This special crystal is coded with the secrets of life.
This crystal is to be used on the
surface of your home.
Use this crystal to bring you back
into the Ocean's Consciousness,
returning to this world anytime you wish.
You can communicate with me anytime you wish,
simply by thought or through your dreams.
I am always with you.
Use this crystal to bring and share
our messages of love,
life and true understanding to our planet.
Thank you for allowing us to share
our world with you.
It is now time for you to return to your world."

****

Ascending back to where time exists,
passing back through the energy vortex,
spiraling up through the colors and
sounds of the oceans,
back up the path that we traveled on,
back to the path to where I started,
back to where the journey all began.
Namaka nudges me back to shore.
I lovingly embrace him and thank him
for sharing his world through his eyes.

****

Feeling myself returning to my body, I became aware of my surroundings. I was sitting on the beach of Polihale. Looking out into the ocean, I saw the shadows of a pod of dolphins swimming away into the ocean. Adjusting back into my normal state, I was overwhelmed with feelings of passion.

Reflecting privately on my inner dream journey, I came to the realization that I was living a life focused on security and survival. I was living **my** life through fear. My inner journey open**ed** my eyes to my own fears, helping me discover that I was not as limited as I thought I was. My boundaries are more expansive and flowing than I believed. My passion was this great power of love ... my passion was limitless. Contemplating my new-found feeling of personal freedom, I realized that I was holding something in my right hand. I opened my hand to see what it was. My eyes lit up at the sight of a beautiful crystal glowing in purple and green hues.

chapter four

A DOLPHIN PORTRAIT

Let me paint a visual picture of the dolphins. Some regard dolphins as just another fish, but they are not! They are cetaceans, warm-blooded marine mammals. Marine means that they live in the ocean. Mammals, unlike fish, have live young instead of eggs and nurse their young. Dolphins also have hair. Dolphins inhabit rivers and oceans throughout the world. They come in five freshwater and thirty saltwater varieties. Dolphins travel in "pods" numbering anywhere from handfuls to thousands, depending on the variety.

Twentieth-century naturalists say that dolphins are land mammals who long ago chose to return to the sea, and oddly enough, x-rays of dolphin flippers show

vestigial hand bones. The National Audubon Society reported that fossil remains of dolphin-like animals that lived in the sea 60 million years ago have been discovered!

Here are a few interesting facts about the dolphins. Although dolphins live in the sea, they breathe air. Dolphins can focus in both air and water because they have strong eye muscles capable of changing their lens shape to receive light rays. Dolphins use their lower jaws in the same way we use our fingers. Dolphins have smooth, soft and sensitive skin that damages easily; however, their skin heals quickly. Their skin somehow changes to streamline their bodies, and discharges oil to make their bodies slippery, allowing them to swim faster. They can swim at up to thirty miles per hour. Flippers and dorsal fins are used for steering while the powerful tail flukes propel the body through the water. Dolphins can grow up to twelve feet long, eat up to fifteen or twenty pounds a day, and can live for fifty years.

If we look back through recorded history, the attraction between dolphins and humans dates back thousands of years. Ancient artifacts include pictures of dolphins. Dolphins have been written about in Greek and Roman mythology. In ancient Greece, dolphins were sacred to Apollo, God of the Sun and the intellect. In France, the King's eldest son bore the title "Dauphin," the French word for dolphin, until the middle of the 19th century. One of the early ruling families from southeastern France had a symbol of a dolphin in its coat of arms. Aristotle, the famous Greek philosopher and writer, wrote about gentle dolphins allowing children to play with them and ride on their backs through the ocean. For centuries, sailors have regarded the presence of dolphins near ships as a sign of a smooth voyage and exceptional good luck.

There are numerous books written about dolphins. Countless stories have been told throughout the centuries. Periodicals and articles appear in scientific and popular literature. Informative and scientifically researched stories about how dolphins have saved humans have been written. In the New Age arena we are seeing more "channeled" dolphin books, stories on future interspecies communication with dolphins, stories about humans who came in contact with them and had a mystical connection. Dolphin swim programs, healing centers and birth centers are now emerging.

Doctors in Russia have been experimenting with underwater birthing for years. It is believed that matching water temperatures with the natural womb temperature produces a softer birth that reduces shock to the new infants. Dr. Motha, who runs the Center for Natural Medicine in London, explained that "dolphins provide the optimal conditions for natural [human] childbirth. They transmit sonar signals which calm the woman in the best possible way and help her give birth quietly, without unnecessary pain and — most important of all — with no trauma to the infant."[2]

As for dolphin "intelligence," there is much we do not know. Humans have tried to discover the consciousness of dolphins through scientific methods. Researchers go down into the water to try to learn their language and to find out why they can move more skillfully than a submarine and perceive underwater obstacles better than sonar.

There have been many documented reports on dolphin intelligence in captivity. Here are some of those reports:

- August 10, 1991: the *Montreal Gazette* cited some instances of dolphin intelligence in captivity.[3]

  Dolphin A learns to get food by performing intricate maneuvers.

  Dolphin B is then allowed to swim. Dolphin B performs the same maneuvers perfectly, first time out.

  Conclusion: Dolphin A told Dolphin B what to do.

- Instructed to "hoop-through," a dolphin leaps through a hoop as it has been trained to do. "Person-through!" the trainer says suddenly.

  The dolphin, never having heard this phrase before, tries to nudge the trainer through the hoop.

  This suggests that dolphins can conceptualize.

- January 1993, the *Smithsonian* magazine reported on the research of psychologist Louis Herman, a University of Hawaii professor, perhaps the nation's most widely respected dolphin communication researcher.[4] Herman developed two artificial languages, one using gestures and the other sounds, to test the dolphins' intelligence. From the results of his research, Herman is convinced dolphins are highly cognitive creatures. One example of his research verified that the captive dolphins he worked with correctly answered the question, "Is there a Frisbee in the pool?" Another example exemplified how the captive dolphins also understood the difference between a request to carry a person to a surfboard in the pool and a request to take the surfboard to a person. Herman concluded from thirty years of research that the dolphins he worked with performed some of the most complex behaviors ever achieved.

- In the March /April 1991 edition, *Sea Frontiers* magazine cited an example of dolphin intelligence.[5] This involved two captive dolphins intent upon extracting a moray eel from a rocky crevice in their tank. One of the dolphins captured a scorpion fish and, with the fish in its mouth, poked at the eel's rear end with the fish's poisonous spine. The moray eel fled from its haven only to be captured by the second dolphin stationed at the opposite end of the hole.

* * * *

As for the dolphins' minds and how they view life, there is so much we do not yet know. Scientists have been researching and studying dolphins for years. They base their research on human standards. Can these scientific theories provide a complete, definitive description of their reality? How can we even compare the human mind to the dolphin mind? Our worlds are so different. We have no understanding of living in their world as much as they have of living in our world. The dolphins have a different way of life. We should reflect on the dolphins just as they are, not from a scientific perspective but as equal counterparts existing and sharing the same universe with us.

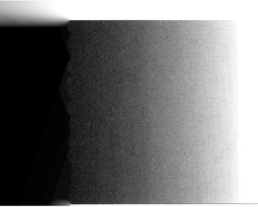

Dolphins are playful
and 'full of fine spirits'
. . . if you can withstand
three cheers at the
sight of dolphins
gamboling off a ship's bow,
then heaven help ye;
the spirit of
godly gamesomeness
is not in ye.

—HERMAN MELVILLE
Moby Dick

chapter 5—

DOLPHIN

MESSAGE

CONNECTION

ONE:

ONE MIND = HARMONY

SOUND CONNECTION

Dolphin Message:

Dolphins use sound and feelings to find food, communicate, maneuver through water and "heal."

Dolphins use sonar as their form of communication. For years, researchers have known that dolphins use sonar beams to navigate the murky depths of the ocean. In fact, in 1992, researchers at the University of California at Santa Cruz used a computer model to study how the skull and network of air sacs inside a dolphin's head act as an acoustical mirror to focus sonar beams.[6]

Let me describe how the dolphins use their sonar. As dolphins swim through the water, they move their heads back and forth (to scan objects). They send out a series of clicks and other sounds which echo, or reverberate, back from fish and other underwater objects in their path. The dolphins then listen to the reflected sounds. They can tell what the objects are, how far away they are and in what direction they are moving. Scientists believe that the echoes travel through the dolphin's lower jaw to the inner ear and are then transmitted to the brain. Using sonar, dolphins are able to find food, communicate, and maneuver through murky waters.

Dolphins are intelligent creatures. Their patterns of reasoning, behavior and interaction with humans have received much attention in research. Interestingly enough, researchers are finding that dolphins even help bring autistic children out of their shells. They attribute this to the dolphins' ability to scan other creatures with their built-in sonar.

Researchers have been conducting

numerous dolphin swim therapy programs for years. One of the most popular dolphin swim therapy centers is in Grassey Key, Florida: "Dolphins Plus. " At Dolphins Plus the emphasis is on research. Dolphins at the center are not there to perform shows nor to entertain people. At this center, dolphins are free to swim out to sea if they choose. Whatever interaction there is with humans at this center is strictly at the dolphins' choice.

At one of these swim sessions, Betsy Smith, a sociologist at Dolphins Plus, noticed that her mentally retarded brother showed improved mental agility after one of the swim sessions with the dolphins. After a bit more experimentation, she discovered the dolphins worked especially well with children. Smith remarked, "As soon as I put a handicapped child in the water, this dolphin relaxes, becomes very different, very, very quiet and calm and will stay with and work with that child as long as it takes. The twelve dolphins who live here have helped dozens of children. That's part of what we call their

'altruistic behavior.'"[7]

There are numerous documented stories about the dolphins' ability to "see" with sonar and how they seem to be able to detect physical abnormalities in people:

- In 1991, *American Health* published an article on Dr. Thomas White, a Business Ethics professor of Rider College in New Jersey.[8] For several years, Dr. White had taken groups of his students to the Dolphin Research Center in Grassey Key, Florida. The first time the professor visited the Center, two parents arrived carrying their blind child. When they went into the water, Tursi, a dolphin with a missing eye who usually did not participate in the swims, immediately came over. Tursi then made noises so the child would know exactly where she was.

- The *Atlanta Journal and Constitution* reprinted a study published in the *Journal of Clinical and Abnormal Psychology* by psychologist David Nathanson, a professor of educational psychology at Florida International University.[9] He conducted a dolphin/child special education program at the Dolphin Research Center in Florida. He spent six months teaching six retarded boys between 2 and 6 years of age everything from the alphabet to complete words, using dolphins both as stimulus and reinforcement. When he compared the speed at which they learned to that of the children he worked with in the classroom, he discovered that the children in the dolphin study learned two to ten times faster. At the 1988 24th International Congress of Psychology in Sydney, Australia, he went as far as to state that these findings conclusively demonstrate that dolphins can enhance the attention span of mentally handicapped children and thus increase the rate of learning. However, he had no explanation as to exactly how this happened.

- In the Fall of 1990, *Shaman's Drum* shared a story which graphically illustrates how dolphins use their sonar to teach and guide.[10] Loyd Burguss of Dolphins Plus tells of a woman who had come to swim with the dolphins for the first time. As soon as she got into the water, they all came over, sounding their sonar and gently butting against her chest and shoulder area. This went on for the entire time she was in the water. The following week, during a routine medical exam, a tiny tumor was discovered in the exact area of the dolphins' focus. Burguss believes the dolphins may have discovered the tumor with their sonar, and tried to call attention to it.

Meanwhile, captive dolphin experiments in therapy and communication continue. Australian psychologists now also use wild dolphins to treat children with cerebral palsy, and a group called the International Dolphin Watch in Great Britain is currently working with wild dolphins to help cure patients with depression.

Dr. Schull, a scientist and expert on animal behavior who completed a study on the mind of the dolphin, explains it simply, "If you realize that these are thinking, feeling, perhaps self-aware animals, you realize that they have a much deeper kind of relationship to you. They can perceive very fine variations in hardness and texture and size using their healing abilities alone. They can read a human being in the water. Given what we know about sonar, there's reason to suspect that they may be able to use their sonar to perceive things that are going on within the skin, the same way that physicians now use ultrasound in order to get a look at fetuses in the womb."[11]

Many scientific and not-so-scientific studies have tried to discover the boundaries of dolphin intelligence to attempt to explain the uplifting effects they have on the human spirit and to explore the apparently mutual fascination between human and dolphin.

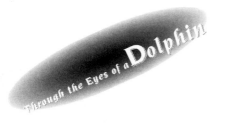

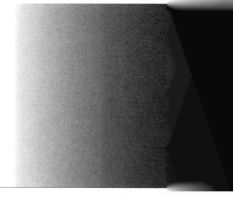

There are still some experiences that defy rationalization and contact with dolphins seems to be among them.

David Nathanson, the Miami-based doctor mentioned earlier, who directed the dolphin/child special education program, used dolphin swim therapy for children with downs' syndrome, cerebral palsy, head and spinal injuries and cancer.[12] Nathanson explained, "Just being in the water helps lower blood pressure and decelerates the heart rate, causing a relaxing response essential for increasing attention. The dolphins are non-judgmental, and the kids love touching them and interacting with them. The positive reinforcement is very powerful. In most cases, the experience gets the children highly motivated. They get kick-started."

Horace Dobbs, a dolphin specialist, describes his research into the uplifting effect dolphins can have on human mood. Dobbs argues that "Getting into the sea with one is enough to raise the spirits of even the most darkly depressed. Wild dolphins have a mysterious, almost evangelical way of reassuring you that somebody loves you."[13]

* * * *

Humans have light to see. Dolphins have sonar. Just as dolphins use sound in echolocating, we use sound in medical examinations. Ultrasound, inaudible to the human ear, is used to take pictures of a baby growing in a mother's womb. Dolphins use sonar to find food, communicate and maneuver through the waters. Dolphins also use sonar to heal people suffering from autism, depression and other mental illnesses. Nobody really knows why it works ... but it does. Is there some kind of communication taking place here?

SOCIAL CONNECTION

Dolphin Message:
**Dolphins are socially and mutually
"inter"dependent on each other.**

Dolphins are social beings. Some travel alone, but nearly all dolphins live in groups. Family groups combine to move about the oceans in schools of hundreds of dolphins. Dolphins swim, play and hunt for food in family groups. Wild bottlenose dolphins range freely and travel as much as 100 miles a day. Members of the group also help protect each other from sharks.

The following stories illustrate that dolphins are truly social beings:

- Jacques Cousteau, of the Cousteau Society, observed that the most obvious conclusion they reached in the course of their experiments was that the dolphins are group animals.[14] According to Cousteau, dolphins are utterly incapable of living alone; with no companionship, they are extremely unhappy and do not adapt to captivity. Left alone they are lethargic and remain inactive. The Cousteau Society noted several incidents in which the dolphins smashed their heads against the pool wall. They believed that this particular dolphin behavior, bearing a remarkable resemblance to suicide, was due to loneliness. But as soon as the dolphins were given a companion, they sprang to life again.

- The *Smithsonian* magazine recounts a story about Richard O'Barry, the famous dolphin trainer for the popular 1960's television series, "Flipper."[15] O'Barry previously captured dolphins in the wild and trained them to perform at the Miami Seaquarium. Five of these dolphins were also used in "Flipper." In 1970,

Kathy, O'Barry's favorite "Flipper" dolphin and a seven year performer, died in his arms. When the TV series had ended, Kathy had been retired to a small steel tank that limited her contact with the other dolphins. O'Barry believed that Kathy committed suicide — for he knew that every breath a dolphin takes is a conscious effort, and Kathy just stopped breathing. O'Barry believes Kathy died of a broken heart.

- Dr. John Lilly, a neurologist credited with starting the whole dolphin movement, also observed the dolphins to be socially and mutually interdependent.[16] He reported a time in which a dolphin being delivered to an oceanarium struck his head on the side of the pool as he was being let in. He was knocked out of consciousness, and dropped to the bottom. The other dolphins then pushed the unconscious dolphin to the surface and held him there until he began to breathe again.

* * * *

Dolphins exist not by virtue of necessary relation. Dolphins exist as beings interconnected, socially and mutually interdependent, not independent. Could it be that in order to live in harmony on the planet, we must experience ourselves not just as solitary human beings? Are the dolphins trying to show us that in order to live in peace we must open ourselves up to this group mind, this communal consciousness?

Mind in the Waters, a book on Whale and Dolphin Consciousness, explains how the dolphin consciousness may be transferred.[17] Dolphin culture may be transmitted in a way similar to the way a traditional indigenous human tribe transmits knowledge: through folk tales and legends. Individuals memorize these stories and then pass them on to the next generation, which in turn memorizes them and passes them on. The immediate and fixed storage capacity necessitated by such a learning method would seem to require a very large brain. Our writing, printing, and similar ways of storing memory outside our brains free us from much of the necessity of memorization. The dolphins must, as it were, remember everything, since they have no libraries, files or writing, or language in any form other than their vocal one.

Scientists describe the human and dolphin brains as similar; however, the folds in the dolphin cortex are more highly developed. John Lilly reports that the brain of the bottlenose dolphin is about 1700 grams, while a human brain weighs about 1450 grams.[18] Yet, the relative brain weight per unit body length of the dolphin is about 200 grams per foot for our 240 grams per foot.

* * * *

It looks like the dolphin's brain is designed for a strong group mind, a conscious connection wherein many minds are linked together. Perhaps our human communal consciousness can also enable us to communicate everything "all at once," creating a group mind in constant harmonious contact with all.

THOUGHT
AND
FEELING
CONNECTION

Dolphin Message:
Dolphins use the vibrations
of their thoughts and feelings
to communicate.

Scientists are learning how dolphins use a wide range of sounds to communicate. Peter Tyack, a scientist at Woods Hole Oceanographic Institution, claims that each dolphin has its own "signature whistle."[19] Dolphins use signature whistles, which seem to function like individual names. Among the more than thirty dolphin species worldwide, herds can number over a thousand strong — and these signature whistles enable one member to tell others who and where it is. Dolphins, in other words, unlike any other species except humans, have names.

Robert MacKnowski, director of Project Interlock, an international group documenting dolphin encounters in the wild, once took the microphone on a pleasure cruise headed up Kauai's Na Pali Coast. MacKnowski asked a group of unsuspecting tourists to help him beckon dolphins by visualizing them leaping into the air. Eighteen minutes later by his watch, a dozen spinner dolphins arrived in pairs, chasing the bow of the boat. Straight ahead, a lone spinner dolphin shot into the air, completed a triple gainer, and slipped neatly back into the sea.[20]

In August of 1994, I was in Kauai and took one of the Zodiac raft cruises that headed up Kauai's Na Pali Coast. I asked the captain the chances of seeing dolphins on this trip. He replied without a blink of his eyes, "One out of a hundred trips." Disappointed with his answer, I began to visualize dolphins playing in the ocean. A few minutes later, dozens of dolphins arrived, headed towards the raft. The captain turned around and gave me a shocked look. I shrugged my shoulders and returned to focus on the delightful show the dolphins were giving us.

* * * *

Dolphins use their feelings to communicate. I was taught that feelings about people and events are considered personal issues. I often considered my inner emotional states my private issues. I thought it was best to keep them separate from my actions. I was programmed to believe that the intelligent way to make important decisions is to "keep my feelings out of it." Now it begins to seem that my thinking cannot be separated from my feelings.

The problem I see is my desire to bypass that which is difficult in order to avoid "feeling" my way through. I have accumulated so many layers of pain clogging my spiritual body that my emotional body now demands release. By feeling, I can communicate to my emotional body which then connects to my spiritual body; I can also communicate with others, interconnecting with a communal consciousness: this group mind.

In order to obtain a higher consciousness in this lifetime, I will have to alter my feelings to engage sufficient power capable of helping me be a part of a world outside of myself. Feelings can help us to experience a greater aliveness in this reality. The act of feeling can also connect us to humanity. If people are only out for themselves and feel no connection with their fellow humans, there can be no interaction. Interaction seems to be the natural way of being interconnected — having no separations, but blending the past and future into a continual oneness.

The dolphins' communal consciousness serves as their language, therefore, it must also act as their memory. "To communicate all at once, using a non-verbal language" would be my definition of telepathy. Dolphins communicate through overwhelming feelings and experiences.

Everything is in motion, everything vibrates, nothing is at rest. Everything, even our thoughts and feelings, must have its corresponding rate mode of vibration. So, like a musical tone, I am able to reproduce it by pressing a key on a piano, causing it to vibrate at a certain rate. Merely through effort and will, my mental states can be produced. The dolphins use thoughts and feelings to communicate. Thought and feeling connection can explain the phenomena of "telepathy."

This non-verbal language is what I use to explain my imagination, how I interpret the music I hear, how I visualize art I see, how I express rhythm when I dance. It's so simple. No logical explanation is needed. All I have to do is open my mind to the realities that can only be explained from within my heart.

The dolphins use feelings to create "interconnection" with all. We, too, can use our feelings to create "interconnection" with all. We, too, can create a higher group consciousness — one group mind bringing harmony to our earth.

When they

look you in the eye,

you feel you've been seen,

down to the bottom

of your soul . . .

They're very good Buddhists.

They're very here, now.

—BETH GAWAIN

57

chapter 6—

DOLPHIN

MESSAGE

CONNECTION

TWO:

AWAKE = AWARE

BREATH AWARE

Dolphin Message:

The dolphins
are conscious breathers,
remaining awake and aware.

Dolphins do not sleep as we do. Jacques Cousteau's twenty-five years of studies verify that a dolphin cannot sleep for more than five to six minutes at a stretch without the threat of drowning.[21] Dolphins in the water are not subject to the effects of gravity or weight, needing less sleep than humans do. Cousteau observed that it appears that the dolphin, in a state of half-sleep, sinks slowly downward in the water, then rises again without ever losing consciousness. The dolphins' breathing, unlike our own, is not automatic and unconscious.

The dolphins' blowhole is a nostril used for breathing at the surface while a powerful muscle closes it when they are underwater. Since their blowholes are on top of their heads, dolphins need to surface only for a short time, breathing in and out rapidly. Their lungs are not very large, yet they breathe deeply and efficiently. When they are surfacing, their hearts beat two to three times faster than when diving, increasing blood flow to their lungs. Upon diving, their lungs collapse and their heart rate decreases, enabling them to adjust to great pressure.

Scientifically it is known that dolphins make better use of their breathing capacity than humans do.[22] A dolphin's lung is relatively the same size as our own. Every time they take a breath, dolphins replace far more air in their lungs than we do. Dolphins extract more of the oxygen from the lungs. They are able to hold more oxygen in the tissue of their muscle. When they dive, their hearts beat far more slowly. The dolphins have a kind of priority system for supplying the brain with unused blood, and so delay the stimulus to take the next breath. Each normal breath is worth six times as much to the dolphin as one of ours is to us.

There are breath-hold divers who easily and naturally expand their lungs like the dolphins. *People* magazine recounted a story about Jacques Mayol, the greatest free diver in recorded history.[23] In 1983, at the age of 56, Mayol, aided by a pair of noseclips and a sixty-six pound weight, dove straight down into the Mediterranean to a record 345 feet (roughly the equivalent span of a 30 story building). Drawing on a lung capacity of about seven quarts (the average for an athlete is about four), Mayol held his breath for three minutes and 15 seconds. Mayol had trained himself through breath control and yoga to hold his breath.

* * * *

Controlling and disciplining the breath is said to be a key to achieving "higher consciousness." More and more people are participating today in these alpha state processes. Ecstasy Breathing is a concept intended to achieve a new spiritual plane through a variety of breathing techniques. Rebirthing is a breathing technique designed to put you in another state of being, so you can remember your own birth or a birth from one of your past lives. I have personally participated in such practices as meditation, hypnosis, visualization, and Tai Chi, which emphasize control and discipline of the breath.

Voluntary breathing oxygenates our brain and stimulates endorphin release that not only gives us pleasure but enhances our state of awareness by moving us into a more relaxed alpha state. The alpha state definitely differs from the state in which I spend most of my waking hours. Some people use certain drugs to achieve this altered state. Others use various techniques designed to focus their attention in ways which are different from their everyday manner of being.

One cannot presume that the exact same state of consciousness is standard for everyone, or that we all experience altered states in the same way. The nature of my consciousness at any particular time would probably depend on the focus of my attention. When I enter an altered state using a meditation technique, I bring information and feelings from my subconscious to my conscious, moving myself into a more heightened sense of reality. I feel more peaceful, calm and balanced. By controlling my attention, I can control my consciousness. I then possess enough free psychic energy to be free to observe and analyze my surroundings objectively.

How then does my unconscious deal with the problems or issues I wish to deal with at that time? Is my unconscious mind the inner guide to my psychological and biological blueprint? Do I have this particular problem due to some negative programming from my past that has interfered with the natural processes that regulate within my conscious-

ness? By accepting and letting myself enjoy this altered state, I can allow my body and mind the natural self-regulation to heal and resolve my problems: essential for my psychological growth.

In an altered state I can select any moment and examine what is going on in my mind. I can look at my waking consciousness confronting the truth about myself and accept it without being defensive or frightened. I can enjoy the experience while staying relaxed and alert. I can begin to regard my mind as a friend, rather than as a poorly-programmed computer. Retraining my attention in this way can give me insight and increase my focus.

Dolphins are conscious breathers, making them more conscious and aware. This must mean that they exist primarily in the alpha state. Dolphins, as conscious breathers, exist in a higher state of consciousness. Our breathing is automatic and unconscious. Does this mean the converse is thus true? Are we unconscious and unaware?

I know what it means to be unconscious and to be conscious. If something happens and I am not aware of it, I am not conscious of it. If I am aware of nothing at all, I am unconscious. Consciousness is awareness — awareness of myself, of others, of everything around me. Therefore, everything I do, have done and will do is part of my consciousness. Consciousness makes me more aware of myself, more aware of others and more aware of everything around me. If I am conscious and aware, I can discover the unique perfection of every moment of my life.

Did I really only know myself at the surface and not know my deeper self? Is being in a calm, balanced and harmonious feeling-state essential for clear thinking and conscious function? Bringing relaxation and calm can bring in awareness. I can become more aware of the moment. By directing awareness at myself, I can bring my mind, emotions, senses, body, etc., under control, creating a more creative and harmonious self.

If humanity were more awake and tuned to the rhythms and cycles of life, we would not do the things we do to our environment. If we were more aware of ourselves and our environment, I believe our outlook would change completely. We would be much more caring about each other and our environment. By replacing this non-awareness with awareness, I will now observe more of the details of my life — plus experience a deeper connectedness with nature.

TUNED IN TO LIFE

Dolphin Message:

Dolphins are tuned to the rhythms and cycles of life.

The earth has a magnetic field. This field is determined by the magnetic features of the soil and rock beneath the land surface of the ocean floor. Scientists think that dolphins have these magnetic senses to "read" (like reading a map) these features as though they were "hills" (higher magnetic fields) and valleys (lower magnetic field). These magnetic hills and valleys have been produced by the movements of the continents over millions of years. They form "paths" in the ocean, like giant "freeways." When dolphins travel on these freeways they know in which direction they are going, because there is always a hill on one side and a valley on the other.[24]

Dolphins transmit sound and feelings over vast distances as a form of communication. Their sensitive skins electrify with even the slightest alterations in their surroundings. Their heightened sense of awareness is natural and not artificially induced like ours, thus they are very tuned to what is happening around them.

Dolphins live in nature outside our artificially tailored world. We cushion and safeguard ourselves from unpredictable weather conditions, in houses and buildings, losing touch with the rhythm of nature. We become unaware of the subtle effects that occur all around us, the coming of nightfall, the shifting of the tides.

Perhaps this state of "unawareness" led society to create our ecological imbalances. Unfortunately our society usually makes decisions of economic policy without any consideration for social and environmental cost or consequence. Just as we may become ill when exposed to environmental hazards, the dolphins too can succumb to toxic chemicals and wastes. Dolphins are dying in increasing numbers from diseases because their immune systems are collapsing.

A mysterious epidemic, similar in its effects to human AIDS, has been reported everywhere. Remember the distressing news in 1987 regarding the numerous dead bodies of bottlenose dolphins that washed up on the New Jersey shore? By March of 1988, 700 bottlenose dolphins from the New Jersey shore down to the Florida shores died. Whale scientist Dr. Roger Payne believes that this breakdown in the dolphin immune system is not due to a virus but to chemical pollutants.[25] Payne believes that PCBs (polychlorinated biphenyls) and other related organohalogens — chemicals that cause tumors, hormone imbalances, genetic deformities and collapse of the immune systems in many species — have been regularly dumped, legally and illegally, in our oceans. Recent research shows concentrations of PCBs in whales and dolphins are between five and twenty times the level that would classify them as toxic waste in the United States.

* * * *

Our earth's overall health is now threatened because of society's unfortunate divisions between economy, social environment and "unawareness." We must go beyond this physical existence, for we and other beings on the planet could become extinct within a surprisingly short time due to massive food shortages, disease and environmentally caused hazards.

The mysterious virus which we call AIDS is a similar version of the breakdown of our global immune system (gaps in the ozone layer, global warming, etc.). If the earth is allowed to deteriorate further, AIDS will be only one problem virus among many. Our ecological imbalances reflect the earth's condition — our planet's overall health is threatened!

All living organisms are living systems. So we should emphasize the whole rather than mere parts. It's like analyzing a tree separately — leaves, branches, trunk, roots — losing sight of the "tree" that gives them being. From the smallest bacterium through the wide range of plants and animals to human beings, all living organisms are living systems. Even parts of our bodies are living systems: the heart, the liver, the kidney and other organs, down to the individual muscles and cells.

We should think of social systems, including family and community, in the same way. All of these systems are "wholes" whose specific structures arise from the interaction and interdependence of their parts. Each member of a given species is an independent being as well as a member of a larger organism.

The world is a reflection of our thoughts and beliefs. The only way I see to ensure global peace and harmony would be for everyone to heal their own minds and think positively. If we remove all thoughts of fear, greed, scarcity, lack and disease from our minds, we can create a world of peace and plenty.

The earth is a beautiful gift that has been given for humanity and beyond. We have been given the power and will to create a beautiful future. Have we chosen a future of pain and suffering by unconsciously destroying our earth? The earth is not pre-destined to be destroyed, but it does require a great deal of healing now, for all beings sharing the earth are suffering and in pain.

There is a traditional American Indian saying, "They who walk with a good balance carry the law within their heart." In other words, I must learn to relate and live in harmony with others and the earth. We need to achieve this sense of harmony with all life, understanding the "Spirit of Being" that manifests itself in all living things.

Dolphins are
kind of the American Indians
of the ocean ...
We're doing everything to them
that we've done to the Indians,
including take away their environment,
take away their freedom ...
what a payback.
Dolphins are
one of the few wild animals
that insist
on maintaining
a good relationship with us.

—RICK TROUT
dolphin consultant

75

chapter 7—

DOLPHIN

MESSAGE

CONNECTION

THREE:

LIVE + LOVE = LIFE

UNCONDITIONAL LOVE

Dolphin Message:

Dolphins express the true meaning of unconditional love.

Today dolphin performances thrill thousands at marine parks. A lot of people feel amazed around dolphins. That is why hundreds of captive dolphins are on display across the country for our pleasure. Dr. John Lilly confirms what marineland personnel have been demonstrating for many years — that dolphins, even when cruelly treated, will not attack human beings.[26] He finds this difficult to believe, since dolphins will attack sharks and kill them. Physically, dolphins are quite capable of tearing or biting an arm or a leg off of a person, and even causing internal injuries by ramming a person's body.

However, Dr. Lilly claims there is no record of these mammals ever having injured a human, even when mistreated.

If we look back through recorded history, it is obvious that dolphins have been saving humans throughout our shared existence on the planet. Arion, a Greek poet who lived about 2,700 years ago, is said to have been saved from the sea by a dolphin when he was thrown overboard by sailors. Though the ancients knew the dolphins well and wrote about how they saved humans, it would seem that we are only now rediscovering these remarkable beings.

Here are a few recent, documented stories about dolphins saving humans:

- August of 1990, Newsday related a story on Dave Miller, 45 year old project manager for a golf course construction company.[27] Miller went fishing with two friends thirty miles off Myrtle Beach, South Carolina, when their boat sprang a leak and capsized. The three spent 29 unnerving hours in the water before the Coast Guard scooped them up.

On three occasions they were circled by sharks, from small hammerheads to a nine-foot Great White. Each time, a group of dolphins materialized and swam interference for the strangers. The project manager vividly recalls the picture of the Great White's eye rolling as it swam by soon after another school of dolphins arrived. They remained for about five minutes, swimming in-between the men and sharks as if someone had sent them and told them they were needed to help at this particular time. The manager and his friends realized that the only time the dolphins appeared was when the men were really in trouble.

- The *Montreal Gazette* recalls a story in 1983 when a helicopter pilot crashed in the Java Sea.[28] Dolphins pushed his rubber raft to Borneo — a journey of eight days and nine nights. Dolphins appear to empathize with the desperate. In1978, dolphins reportedly formed a protective ring around a sea lion being attacked by killer whales near the former Soviet Union's Kamchatka peninsula.

- A story in *Boy's Life* magazine recounts the adventure of a boy scout sailing off Waikiki Beach, Hawaii.[29] The boy scout was thrown into the water when his dinghy capsized. A pod of friendly dolphins pushed him back to the dinghy, saving his life.

- Amidst the tragedy of 1992's devastating cyclone in Bangladesh, a story of another breathtaking rescue by a dolphin was reported in the *San Francisco Chronicle*.[30] The Minister for the Environment of Bangladesh informed reporters that a dolphin had rescued a baby swept out to sea from the village of Ukhia by a tidal wave during the height of the cyclone. People from the village witnessed the dolphin holding the baby in its mouth, delivering the baby back to shore.

* * * *

As discussed earlier, due to their sensitivity to humans, dolphins are being utilized as motivational 'tools' in working with mentally handicapped children. I fondly remember the 1993 broadcast of ABC's "Primetime Live."[31] The show aired a clip entitled "Joey's Best Friend," in which John Quinones of "Primetime" traveled to Dolphins Plus. Scientists at the research center have discovered that compassion, particularly in work with physically or mentally impaired children, can heal.

Joey was born with a rare congenital heart disease that robs the body of oxygen. By the time he was three years old, Joey had undergone three open heart surgeries. Following the last operation, he suffered a stroke. The left side of Joey's body was paralyzed. He was blind in his left eye and lay in a coma for eight days.

Although doctors said he might not recover after such a long ordeal, Joey finally came out of the coma. He refused to cooperate with his doctors and physical therapist due to a distrust of humans.

Joey's parents had just about given up hope for Joey's recovery when they heard about Dolphins Plus. When Joey first laid eyes on the dolphins, he was shy and apprehensive. Soon after, however, a friendly dolphin named Fonzie swam up to greet him.

After eight months of dolphin therapy, Joey now lugs a heavy pail of fish to feed his buddy, Fonzie. At one time he was not even able to move a finger on his left hand. He now wiggles it away, for that is the signal that makes Fonzie talk. Yet there were doctors who said Joey would never run, there were doctors who predicted he would always walk with a limp, and there was a speech therapist who stated he would never sing. When Quinones asked Joey to describe what Fonzie had done for him, Joey answered, "He made me feel better." Joey's life has been turned around by a 700-pound playmate.

****

The twelve dolphins who live at the dolphin research center have helped dozens of children. The truth is, dolphins are saving humans at a much greater rate than humans are saving dolphins. Not only do they nudge us ashore when they find us in distress and danger in the open shore, they guide our ships safely through fog and treacherous channels. Not only do they care for each other, they also show a deep sensitivity and caring for us. The dolphins are expressing unconditional love; they care and are truly giving, asking nothing in return.

To the Dolphin Alone,
beyond all other,
Nature has granted
what the best
Philosophers seek:
Friendship with no
advantage.

—PLUTARCH,
1st Century A.D.

85

SACRIFICE FOR COMPASSION

***Dolphin Message*:**
Dolphins sacrifice their bodies to awaken human compassion.

Across the world, every year, humans have been responsible for the slaughter of hundreds of thousands of dolphins. To fishermen, the presence of dolphins usually indicates schools of tuna swimming below. Unfortunately, dolphins caught in the tuna nets drown when they cannot swim to the surface for air. Roughly half a million dolphins die annually from man-made causes, including water pollution in coastal areas and driftnets that are still used in many countries. Japan has no law against killing dolphins for eating. South America kills dolphin for fish bait.

The National Audubon Society points to some disturbing figures regarding dolphin deaths.[32] Since 1960, an estimated six million dolphins have been killed by tuna fisheries in the Pacific. Incredibly, the United States National Marine Fisheries Services in 1972 introduced a quota limit for dolphin safe tuna which allows 20,000 dolphins to be incidentally killed before tuna fishing must be stopped each year. In Japan alone, 50,000 dolphins are killed for food each year.

Jacques Cousteau states that there are certain documented facts which cannot be explained without attributing certain emotional or affective drives to dolphins.[33] He ponders: What is one to think of the dolphin in captivity, who, upon the death of his companion, stubbornly kept the corpse from sinking? Dolphins, too, have sympathetic hearts, capable of human-kindness, if you will.

* * * *

From tragedies, human compassion can be awakened. Remember the aftermath of the devastating earthquake that hit San Francisco in 1989? The media broadcast the news worldwide, affecting even people with no personal concern in the disaster. The world's political and religious differences were put aside. Money, food, and medical supplies from around the world were brought into the San Francisco Bay Area to help bring relief. From tragedy, human compassion was awakened.

Throughout history, dolphins have held a special meaning for people. A variety of forces are destroying the dolphin populations around the world. For the past decade, we have exhibited a genuine interest in working to "Save the Dolphins" from the tuna nets, specifically, and more generally, from exploitation by humans. Our attempt to save the dolphins may all be well and good, but perhaps they are attempting to convey another message. Could it be that they are trying to awaken our compassion through their sacrifices?

I hear numerous stories about dolphins that swim into very shallow water and find themselves stranded on the beach, yet, they are such strong swimmers. What about the thousands of dolphins caught in tuna nets which drown? I have seen dolphins perform magnificent antics at marine parks — can't they just jump out of the nets?

It makes me wonder, do dolphins voluntarily sacrifice their bodies in an attempt to activate our consciousness through visual anguish and despair? Could it be that they allow themselves to be captured, killed and let themselves be our companions as a way of reminding us about our compassion? Through their sacrifice, my compassion is awakened.

Humans are not the only species capable of compassion. Dolphins must relate to one another through a social behavior largely based upon compassion. They never exhibit fear and are always friendly towards us. Not only are they beautiful, strong, and intelligent, they also have sympathetic hearts.

The universe is a place of perfection even amidst the chaos. Each one of us is capable of evolving beyond a survival consciousness, capable of healing our fears and negative beliefs by creating positive ones and awakening our compassionate selves. When love and compassion are open, real transformation can occur, awakening our spiritual being.

FULL
ON
LIFE

Dolphin Message:

Dolphins live deliberately
as all nature does,
full of the energy
of life.

As powerful beings of the ocean, dolphins help me appreciate their ocean world. It is hard not to be impressed by their athletic abilities and clever nature. Performing dolphins are a big part of a growing business. Millions of people visit marine parks all over the country. Among all the marine mammals performing at the marine parks, dolphins seem to hold a special fascination for me.

Mind in the Waters illustrates two stories of the spontaneous playfulness of the dolphins:[34]

- A dolphin in the Bahama Islands apparently invented a retrieving-type game on his own. He picked up a small floating stick and propelled it a distance of ten feet or so. He then swam ahead and retrieved the stick, only to propel it another ten feet. He continued to repeat this activity as he swam in circles. Here is an exhibition of pure spontaneous playfulness!

- A dolphin in Marineland, Florida, found a feather lost by one of the pelicans inhabiting the tank's surface. The dolphin balanced the feather on his nose, flipped it backward and attempted to catch it. Another dolphin then also rushed up to try to catch the feather as it fell. He then raced off, pursued by others who tried to take the feather from him.

* * * *

The dolphins' behavior is not merely playful and meaningless. It is full of purpose. The dolphins are giving life back to the sea that gave them life. The dolphins live "full on life," giving and receiving life's energies. That's what I would call a balanced way of life.

Was I living my life all wrong? Worries of power and control weigh my life down. I am living with no balance, no interchange of life's energies. I should manage, moderate, and balance my intellectual power and knowledge through the wisdom and compassion of my heart and live like the dolphins, "full of energy." I should live a life that is balanced and open to accept the loving embrace of the earth.

I created a life of so much complexity, stress and worry. I am always busy in my real world worrying about my future. I am always wondering what I am going to do or say next. I have to remember my next appointment, meetings, lunch and dinner engagements. I must remember to go to the store, pay my bills, pick up my laundry. My mind is always cluttered with the

details of my daily life. Sometimes I become stressed out by stressing out. I feel like a robot, my life is a continual cycle and pattern repeating the same things over and over again.

Have I skipped over something very crucial and important for my personal, spiritual growth? I seem to have forgotten that I am responsible for myself. I have created my own problems. I was consciously avoiding full responsibility for my own behavior. I cannot blame anyone for my life, for I chose every-thing. I am responsible for myself.

Would it not be easier to live a life of simplicity like the dolphins? Would it not be simpler to live like the dolphins, by living a life "full on being," appreciating life to its fullest?

Life is not something I am supposed to do from time to time when I am not busy doing other things. Life is what I am and what I make it to be. Instead of worrying about life and how I am going to get "there," I should just "be here" and enjoy the journey life has to offer. A simple life of heart.

**I don't know
of any other animal
that is gentle, very playful,
appears to be compassionate
and intelligent,
all in one ...**

**I think that's the nature
of people's attraction:
All the better qualities
we value in other people,
we see in them.**

—TERRY HAWKINS
biologist

95

Epilogue

The word "dolphin" comes from the Greek word "delphi" meaning womb. The womb is where a baby grows before it is born, hence it is the place of life. People of ancient times believed that dolphins had special powers because they came from the ocean — the source of all life. To name a sea-being after the source of life means that the people of that time must have believed the dolphins were very important.

In all the myths and legends that have been passed down through eons of time, the dolphins are most remembered as guides. Jesus was, in fact, depicted as a benevolent dolphin. Ancient art abounds with evidence of the trusting friendship between dolphins and humans. The Minoans of the Mediterranean Island of Crete, thousands of years ago, regarded the dolphin as a symbol of music and joy.

What is it about dolphins that captivates my mind? They have been blessed with an eternal smile, a brain larger than ours, the most acute hearing of any animal, a built-in sonar system and a lovable, adorable image. Their intense eyes express humane compassion and enlightenment.

The mystical connection that I have with the dolphins served to awaken my deep inner self. The dolphins have touched my heart and soul, opened my mind and imagination. The dolphins brought out my creativity, lovingness, compassion and spontaneity. What could be more spontaneous than a dolphin?

Their extraordinary intelligence combined with their harmonious mind and higher consciousness encourages me to explore my own potential. Their unconditional love, sacrifice and joy of being awakens my longing for the same. Dolphins can show us how to manage and moderate our left and right brain through the wisdom and compassion of the heart.

I hope that *Through the Eyes of a Dolphin* has helped to open and touch your hearts through its subtle messages. I truly believe that dolphins are spiritual teachers. They seem to summon us to reawaken. They save us, entertain us, and delight us — offering themselves as our friends. They offer a message of hope for our distressed world. Most of us are closed to messages from the intuitive self, and this, I believe, is the level at which the dolphins are attempting to communicate to us.

The dolphins' consciousness is what we lack and sorely need. They tell us to *"Wake up, lighten up, be freer, play more, life is too short!"* Given the chance, dolphins can enlighten us and show us a different view of being; they see harmony, they experience, they live and love life. The dolphins are intensely conscious of what they are doing ... this is the *"Dolphin Consciousness"* ... expressing a simple but true message of cooperation and intunement with life.

Live as Free as the Dolphins!

Through the Eyes of a Dolphin

DOLPHIN / MARINE MAMMAL
PROJECT CENTERS

- Center for Marine
  Conservation
  1725 DeSales St., N.W.,
  Washington, D.C.
  20036
  (202) 429-5609

- National Marine Mammal
  Laboratory
  7600 Sand Point Way N.E.
  Seattle, Washington
  98115
  (206) 526-4045

- Progressive Animal Welfare
  Society (PAWS)
  P.O. Box 1037
  Lynwood, Washington
  98046
  (206) 742-4142

- Save the Dolphins Project /
  Earth Island Institute
  300 Broadway, Suite 28
  San Francisco, California
  94133
  (415) 788-3666

- The Sea Shepherd
  Conservation Society
  1314 2nd St.
  Santa Monica, California
  90401
  (310) 394-3198

- The Wild Dolphin Project
  21 Hepburn Avenue, Suite 20
  Jupiter, Florida
  33458
  (407) 575-5660

DOLPHIN
PROGRAMS

102

- **Dancing Dolphin Institute**
  Kihei, Maui, Hawaii
  (808) 573-4235

- **DolphINsight**
  Del Mar, California
  (619) 792-0919

- **Dolphins Plus**
  Key Largo, Florida
  (305) 451-1993

- **Dolphin Quest**
  Waikoloa, Hawaii
  (808) 885-1234

- **Dolphin Research Center**
  Grassey Key, Florida
  (305) 289-0002

- **Hawk's Cay Resort and Marina**
  Duck Key, Florida
  (305) 743-7000

- **International Dolphin Watch**
  North Humberside, Great Britain
  44-482-643-403

- **Oceanic Society Expeditions**
  San Francisco, California
  (800) 326-7491

- **Theatre of the Sea**
  Islamorada, Florida
  (305) 664-2431

- **Underwater Explorer's Society**
  Port Lucaya, Grand Bahamas Island
  (800) 992-DIVE

Bibliography

1   Sam Keen and Anne Valley-Fox, *Your Mythic Journey* (Los Angeles: Jeremy P. Tarcher, Inc., 1989), p.11.

2   Andrew Meisels, "Flipper Booted as Midwife, Israel Cuts Cord on Birthing Plan." *Washington Times,* 10 September 1992, sec. Part A, p. A9.

3   Michelle Lalonde, "Dolphin Facts: In an Ocean Full of Dullards, What Good is Such a Brain?" *Montreal Gazette,* 10 August 1991, sec. Science: Earth Matters, p. L-6.

4   David Riley, "Our Love of Dolphins Has Turned into a Questionable Affair." *Smithsonian,* 23 (January 1993): 43-50.

5   Susan H. Shane, "Smarts: Notes On Dolphin Brain Power, Communication Skills and Social Style." *Sea Frontiers,* 34 (March/April 1991): 50-54.

6   Tom Hilchey, "Skull and Air Sacs Tune Dolphin Sonar (University of California at Santa Cruz Dolphin Research)." *New York Times,* 10 November 1992, sec. N, p. B9.

7   "Joey's Best Friend," Prime Time Live (ABC News Transcript), 30 January 1992.

8   Carol Goodstein, "Healers from the Deep."
    American Health: *Fitness of Body & Mind*,
    10 (September 1991): 60-65.

9   "Dolphin Therapy's Leap of Hope for Brain-
    Damaged Boy." *Atlanta Journal and Constitution*., sec.
    D, Features, p. 2.

10 Kim Rosen, "Dancing with Dolphins: Healing
    through Interspecies Connections." *Shaman's
    Drum*, (Fall 1990): 19-24.

11 "Joey's Best Friend," Prime Time Live (ABC News
    Transcript), 30 January 1992.

12 Michael & Patti Schuman, "Getting into the Swim:
    Special Programs Offer a Dolphin's-Eye View of
    Life." *Chicago Tribune*, 18 October 1992, sec. Travel,
    p. 3.

13 Lynn Truss, "Flipper Was Never Like This: Lynn
    Truss Defies Her Fear of the Deep to Test a Theory
    that Dolphins Can Help Cure Depression."
    Independent, 26 August 1990, sec. Sunday Review,
    p. 10.

14 Jacques Y. Cousteau and Philippe Diole, *Dolphins*:
    The Undersea Discoveries of Jacques Yves Cousteau.
    (New York: Doubleday & Co. Inc., 1975), p. 49.

15 David Riley, "Our Love of Dolphins has Turned into a Questionable Affair." *Smithsonian*, 23 (January 1993) 43-50.

16 John C. Lilly, *Man and Dolphin*. (New York: Doubleday & Co. Inc., 1961), p.36.

17 John C. Lilly, *Man and Dolphin*. (New York: Doubleday & Co. Inc., 1961), p. 37.

18 John C. Lilly, *Man and Dolphin*. (New York: Doubleday & Co. Inc., 1961), p. 21.

19 Peter Ola & Emily D'Aulaire, "Playful Genius of the Sea: Dolphins." *Reader's Digest*, 140 (March 1992): 54-59.

20 Lynn Smith, "For Some, Dolphins Bring Spiritual Inspiration." *Los Angeles Times*, 16 August 1989, sec. View, p. 8.

21 Jacques Y. Cousteau and Philippe Diole, *Dolphins: The Undersea Discoveries of Jacques Yves Cousteau*. (New York: Doubleday & Co., Inc., 1975), p. 173.

22 Anthony Alpers, *Dolphins: The Myth and the Mammal*. (Massachussetts: Riverside Press, 1961), p. 63.

23 John Stark & Careth Elling, "From Out of the Big Blue Comes Free-Diving Champ Jacques Mayol." *People*, 19 September 1988, sec. Adventure. p.134.

24 Janelle Heatherly, *Great Creatures of the World:*
Dolphins and Porpoises. (New York: Facts on File, Inc.,
1990), p. 59.

25 David Day, "Mysterious Epidemic Under the Sea:
Scientist Claims Chemicals are Killing Whales and
Dolphins," *Sea Shepard Log,* (First Quarter 1993)
p. 9.

26 John C. Lilly, *Man and Dolphin,* (New York:
Doubleday & Co. Inc., 1961), p. 61.

27 Tom Dunkel, "The Dolphin Mystique: They're
Adored and Applauded, Used and Abused by
Humans. The Relationship Has Made Them a
Metaphor for our Dealings with the Natural World."
Newsday, 12 August 1990, p. 6.

28 Michelle Lalonde, "Dolphins Seem to Empathize
with the Desperate." *Montreal Gazette,* 10 August
1983, sec. Science: Earth Matters, p. L-6.

29 John Sharkey, "Swim with Dolphins." *Boy's Life,* 82
(January 1992) p. 8.

30 "Dolphin Rescue," *San Francisco Chronicle,* 5 June
1992.

31 "Joey's Best Friend," Prime Time Live (ABC News
Transcript), 30 January 1992.

32 "If Dolphins Could Talk" (National Audubon Society Special Video) 1990.

33 Jacques Y. Cousteau and Philippe Diole, *Dolphins: The Undersea Discoveries of Jacques Yves Cousteau,* (New York: Doubleday & Co. Inc., 1975), p. 29.

34 Joan McIntyre, *Mind in the Waters: A Book to Celebrate the Consciousness of Whales and Dolphins.* (New York: Charles Schribner's Sons, 1974), p. 95.

About the Author

Liliana Saca was born and raised in Southern California. She has lived overseas and on both the east and west coasts. She has traveled nationally and internationally extensively. These travels have opened Liliana's eyes and increased her awareness of the world around her.

Although this is Liliana's first book, she is an accomplished self-starter. She has her own unique style, illustrated in her recent workshop in Orinda, California, on Dolphin Magic — an enlightening and informative presentation on the dolphin mystique. The search for herself, along with her years of research, are the foundation upon which she has based her book.

Liliana holds a Bachelor of Science degree in Psychology and a Master of Arts degree in Interdisciplinary Consciousness. Liliana currently lives in San Francisco, California. She presently works for a Bay Area technical consulting firm as Director of Strategic Planning and International Liaison.

111